DINOSAUR
ACTIVITY
BOOK

Andy Passchier
Gemma Barder

ARCTURUS

ARCTURUS

This edition published in 2024 by Arcturus Publishing Limited
26/27 Bickels Yard, 151–153 Bermondsey Street,
London SE1 3HA

Illustrator: Andy Passchier
Author: Gemma Barder
Consultant: Anne Rooney
Designer: Ariadne Ward
Editor: Violet Peto
Design Manager: Jessica Holliland
Managing Editor: Joe Harris

ISBN: 978-1-3988-3608-2
CH010459NT
Supplier 29, Date 1023, PI 00004804

Printed in China

SOARING PTERANODON

This Pteranodon is soaring high above the prehistoric world!

Can you figure out which silhouette is a perfect match?

teh-RAH-no-don

THE DAWN OF THE DINOSAURS

Dinosaurs lived on Earth for around 165,000,000 years. That's a really long time, considering that humans like you and me have only been here for around 300,000 years!

Take a look at the timeline below showing the three main ages of the dinosaurs: Triassic, Jurassic, and Cretaceous. Can you draw a line between the missing dinosaurs and their space on the timeline?

TRIASSIC PERIOD
252 to 201 million years ago

▶ ## JURASSIC PERIOD
201 to 145 million years ago

Plateosaurus
PLAT-ee-oh-SORE-us

Eoraptor
EE-oh-RAP-tuhr

Camptosaurus
KAMP-toe-SORE-us

Diplodocus
dip-LOH-doh-kus

A   B   C

CRETACEOUS PERIOD
145 to 66 million years ago

Megalosaurus

MEG-ah-low-SORE-us

Triceratops

try-SEH-ra-tops

Kentrosaurus

KEN-tro-SORE-us

Ankylosaurus

an-KIH-loh-SORE-us

PUZZLE PIECES

Parasaurolophus lived from 78-80 million years ago in what is now the United States. It was one of the last dinosaurs to roam the Earth. Take a look at this jigsaw puzzle, and see if you can find the missing pieces. Which pieces don't belong?

A   B   C   D   E   F

PA-ra-sore-OL-off-us

EGG HUNT

Did you know that dinosaurs laid eggs? Heyuannia huangi was a fast-moving feathered dinosaur. Its eggs were blue-green.

Which route should this mother take to get back to her nest of eggs?

hay-YEW-a-ni-a HWAN-gi

MUM'S THE WORD

Maiasaura was one of the best dinosaur parents around. They would keep their young with them until they could find their own food.

Can you spot all five differences between these two pictures of a Maiasaura and her young?

MY-ah-SORE-ah

JURASSIC PLANTS

Follow these prehistoric leaves in the order below, before the herbivores gobble them up! There will be one pathway from the top to the bottom of the maze. You can move up, down, left, and right, but not diagonally.

Start

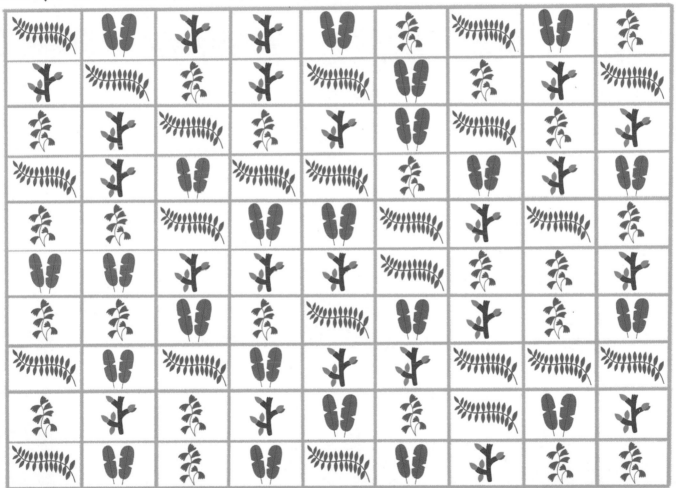

Finish

FOSSIL-DOKU

The reason we know so much about dinosaurs is because of the fossils they left behind. Can you fit each one of these fossils in every row, column, and minigrid?

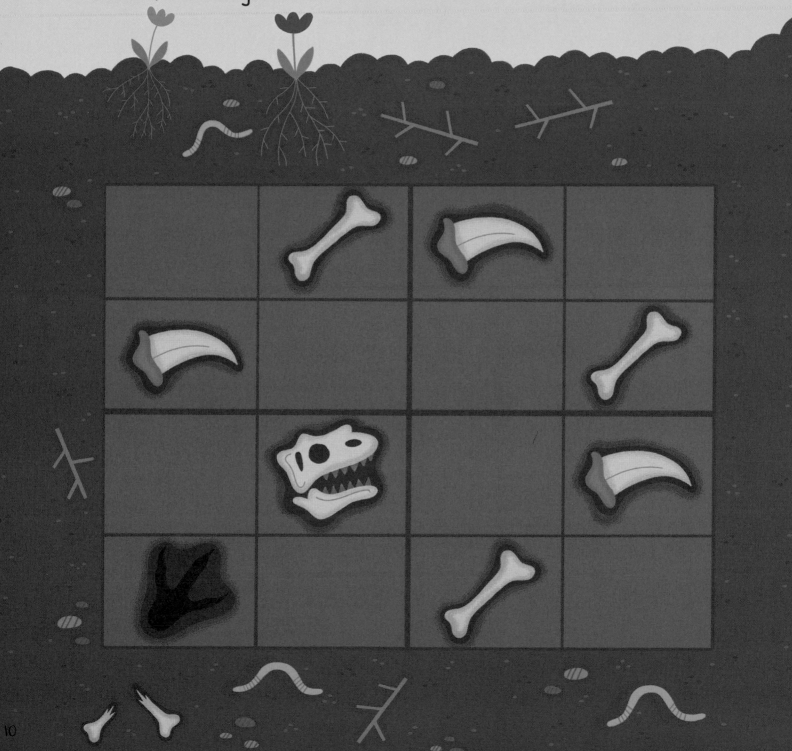

IGUANODON PALS

Iguanodon was a herbivore, meaning it ate only plants. Its skin may have been patterned to help it hide among the trees.

Look at these pictures, and see if you can find three matching pairs of Iguanadons.

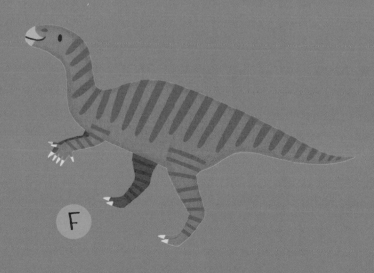

ig-WAH-noh-don

SEARCH AND FIND

Brachiosaurus moved from place to place looking for the tastiest plants.

Take a look at this picture of some wandering Brachiosaurus to see if you can find all the details in the list.

BRAK-ee-oh-SORE-us

 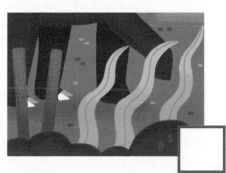 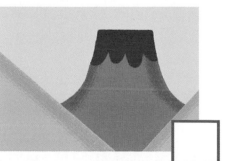

13

MICRO BUT MIGHTY!

Microraptor is one of the smallest dinosaurs ever to have been discovered. How many can you count on this page?

MY-kroh-rap-tuhr

PLOTTING PLESIOSAURUS

Plesiosaurus was a sea-dwelling reptile that lived in the Jurassic period.

Use the directions to follow this Plesiosaurus' route through the ocean. How many fish will she eat along the way?

Start at A1; Up 3; Right 5; Up 2; Left 4; Up 1; Right 3

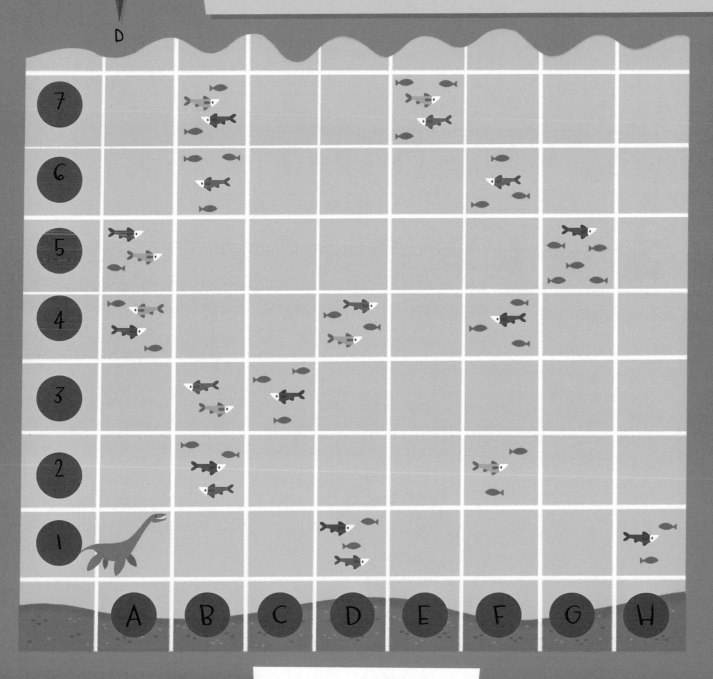

pleh-see-oh-SORE-us

CODEBREAKING

These amazing fossils have been found all over the world. They belonged to a creature that lived underwater more than 66 million years ago and is related to the octopus.

Crack the code to discover the name of this creature!

Codebreaker

E	A	U	P	M	N	O	I	D	T
✛	✿	▼	◻	◼	✳	◗	◉	○	◈

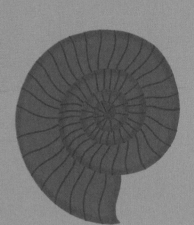

Write your answer here. ↱

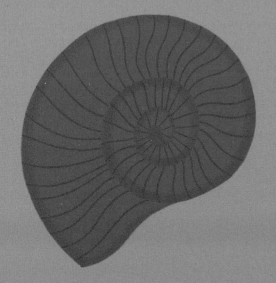

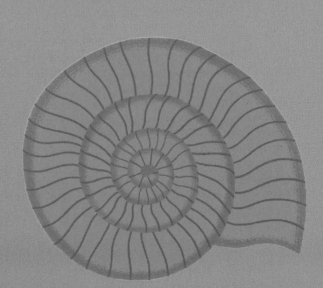

PARASAUROLOPHUS

We know that Parasaurolophus had an unusual head shape. However, we don't know whether the pattern on its skin was bright or dull.

Finish off this picture to show what you think Parasaurolophus looked like.

PA-ra-sore-OL-off-us

TRUE OR FALSE?

Iguanodon lived in the early Cretaceous Period and fed on plants. But what else do you know about this dinosaur?

Look at these facts, and see if you can figure out which ones are true and which are false.

The first fossils to be discovered were their teeth.

T ☐ F ☐

They could jump as high as a house.

T ☐ F ☐

They could swim.

T ☐ F ☐

They each weighed as much as a small truck.

T ☐ F ☐

They only ate brown leaves.

T ☐ F ☐

ig-WAH-noh-don

ODD PSITTACOSAURUS OUT

Psittacosaurus was a small dinosaur from the Cretaceous Period.

Look carefully to see if you can spot which Psittacosaurus is the odd one out.

A

B

C

D

E

F

G

SIT-ak-oh-SORE-us

WHO CAME FIRST ON LAND?

Take a look at all these incredible dinosaurs. Do you know which of them lived the longest time ago?

Figure out the order of when each type of dinosaur lived based on the clues. Then draw them in the boxes below from oldest to most recent.

Achillobator

ah-KILL-oh-bate-or

Diplodocus

dip-LOH-doh-kus

1

2

Longest time ago ▶   ▶

CLUES

- Cryolophosaurus and Plateosaurus lived the longest time ago.
- Achillobator lived less long ago than Diplodocus.
- Cryolophosaurus is not the oldest dinosaur.

Cryolophosaurus

CRY-oh-low-foe-SORE-us

Plateosaurus

PLAT-ee-oh-SORE-us

3

4

▶   ▶   Most recent

GUIDE THE GIRAFFATITAN

Giraffatitans grew to 23 m (over 75 ft), and they are among the tallest dinosaurs ever to be discovered. Like their cousins, Brontosaurus and Diplodocus, they roamed from place to place looking for tasty leaves to munch.

Start

Guide this Giraffatitan through the maze to get to the leaves on the other size.

JEE-raf-ah-TY-tan

Finish

SPEED RACER!

Dromiceiomimus was one of the fastest dinosaurs to have lived, running at nearly 60 kph (40 mph).

Can you find the quickest route for this Dromiceiomimus to take?

dro-MY-see-oh-MIH-muss

Start

A

D

2 seconds

3 seconds

2 seconds

C

E

4 seconds

1 second

B

2 seconds

F

1 second

2 seconds

G

Finish

ANKYLOSAUR ADDITION

Ankylosaurus had a bony "club" at the end of its tail to defend itself against predators. Can you match the equations on the left to their answers on the right?

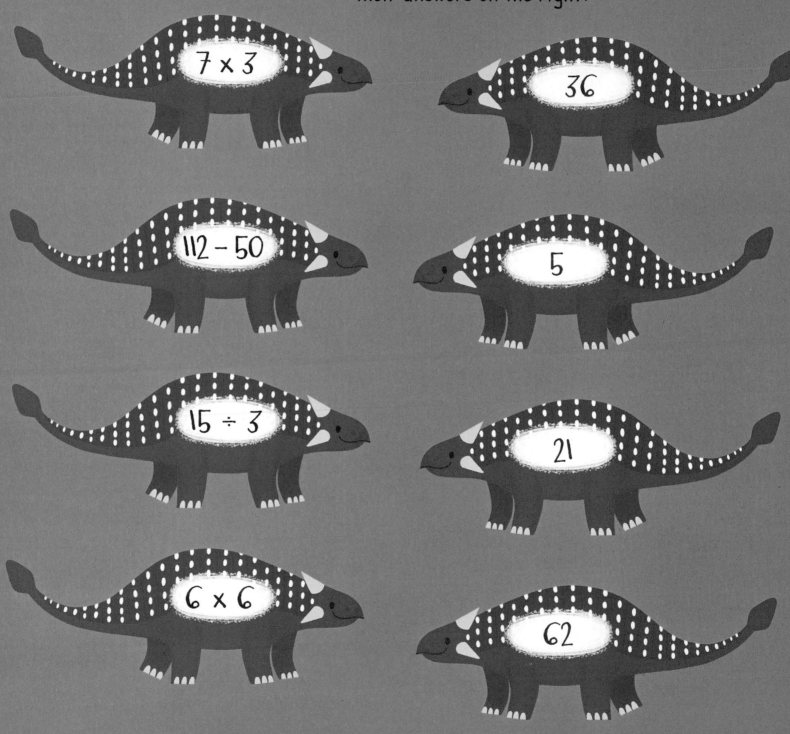

7×3

36

$112 - 50$

5

$15 \div 3$

21

6×6

62

an-KIH-loh-SORE-us

LEAF-PICKER

This young Brachiosaurus is learning which leaves are the tastiest. Can you put this bunch of ginkgo leaves back together again to help him?

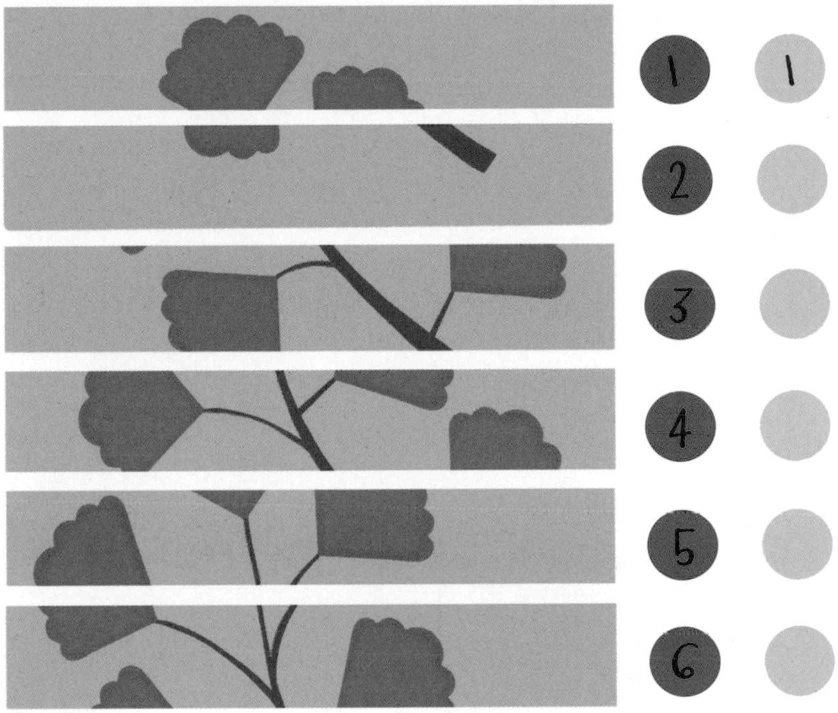

1   1
2
3
4
5
6

BRAK-ee-oh-SORE-us

FIND THE PATH

Fish-eating Spinosaurus roamed in rivers and mangrove forests, looking for tasty food to eat.

Cross out all the odd numbers to find a path of even numbers for the Spinosaurus to cross the marshy river.

Start

5

19

11

6

37

53

17

10

23

29

26

31

3

90

36

7

47

12

41

13

43

SPINE-oh-SORE-us

TEST YOUR MEMORY

Dinosaur scientists have to remember a lot of details
when they are out on a dig. Take a look at this scene for
30 seconds, then turn the page to see what you can remember!

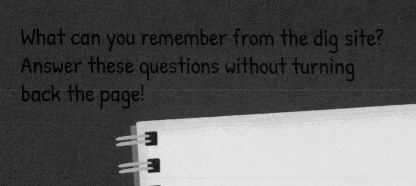

What can you remember from the dig site?
Answer these questions without turning
back the page!

1. How many blue pencils
were there?

2. Was the notebook open
or closed?

3. Was the fossil brush
blue or green?

4. How many bones were
being uncovered?

5. Was the trowel handle red
or yellow?

ODD ELASMOSAURUS OUT!

Elasmosaurus was a marine reptile that lived in the late Cretaceous period. It had one of the longest necks of any prehistoric creature!

Can you spot the Elasmosaurus that isn't quite like the others?

el-LAZZ-moh-SORE-us

EGGS-TRA TRICKY

The largest dinosaur eggs belonged to a dinosaur named Beibeilong. These eggs were 45 cm (18 in) long. The smallest dinosaur eggs ever found were only 18 mm (1/2 in) long!

Follow this pattern of dinosaur eggs from start to finish. You can move up, down, left, and right, but not diagonally.

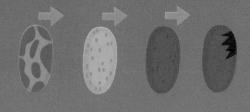

Start

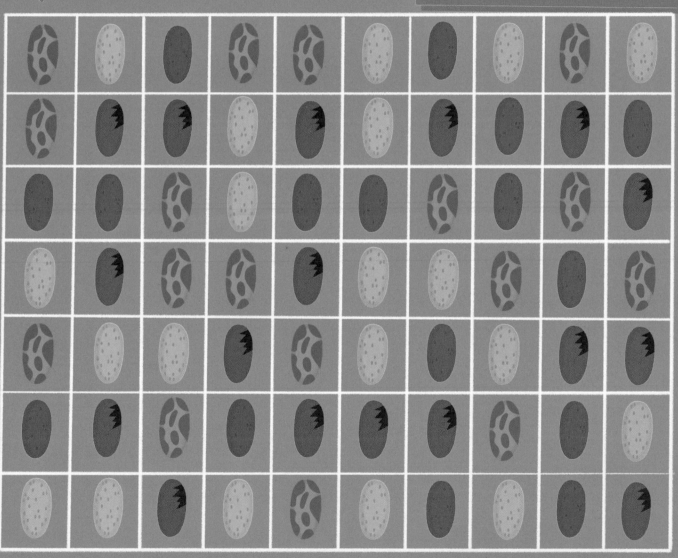

Finish

bay-bay-LONG

WHICH DINOSAUR?

Read the clues to see which type of horned dinosaur is being described.

1. It has more than two horns.
2. Its nose horn is straight.
3. Its frill is divided into two sections.

Triceratops

try-SEH-ra-tops

Chasmosaurus

KAZ-moh-SORE-us

Einiosaurus

EYE-nee-oh-SORE-us

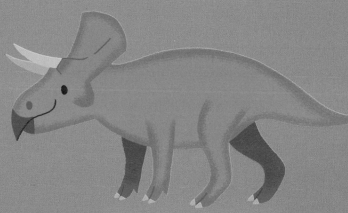

Zuniceratops

ZOO-nee-SEH-rah-tops

SKELETON SWITCH

Although this Champsosaurus looked and acted just like a crocodile, it was actually a crocodile-like reptile that lived in the late Cretaceous Period.

Take a look at this Champsosaurus, then see if you can find its perfect skeleton match below!

1

2

3

4

5

CHAMP-soh-SORE-us

TOOTH OR DARE

Teeth are one of the most common types of dinosaur fossils to be found.

How many of each tooth shape can you count in the jumble below?

Ankylosaurus tooth   Spinosaurus tooth

Match the descriptions to each tooth type to see who ate what!

These long, sharp teeth allowed its carnivorous owner to tear through meat.

These belonged to a herbivore. The small, leaf-shaped teeth were designed for eating plants.

SEARCH THE SEAS!

There are 5 names of prehistoric aquatic reptiles hidden in this grid. Can you find them all?

The names can go forward, backward, vertically, and even diagonally!

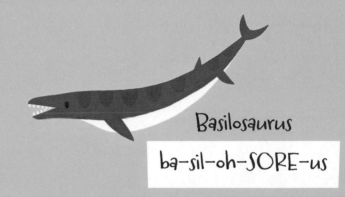

Basilosaurus

ba-sil-oh-SORE-us

Megalodon

meh-GAH-lo-don

P	D	F	G	H	J	T	Y	H	E	J	M
V	L	S	V	B	N	X	G	H	L	K	E
A	I	E	C	A	B	N	H	J	A	U	G
R	C	G	S	S	C	V	B	N	S	L	A
D	H	V	B	I	D	F	G	R	M	S	L
C	T	J	K	L	O	R	T	Y	O	J	O
M	H	A	S	O	C	S	N	H	S	K	D
I	Y	O	L	S	N	M	A	H	A	Y	O
R	O	G	T	A	S	N	M	U	U	T	N
E	S	R	T	U	Y	H	N	M	R	Q	A
B	A	N	M	R	S	D	F	V	U	U	U
N	U	M	A	U	T	I	L	D	S	A	S
E	R	S	M	S	A	E	N	M	H	T	Y
G	U	H	N	U	W	E	R	T	F	H	U
E	S	R	T	R	Y	H	N	M	R	Q	A

Ichthyosaurus

ICK-thee-oh-SORE-us

Plesiosaurus

PLEH-zee-oh-SORE-us

Elasmosaurus

el-LAZZ-moh-SORE-us

TRACE THE TRACKS

Like animals living today, dinosaurs made tracks in soft ground.

Add up the numbers on each footprint trail below. Then match them to the correct total to discover which dinosaur they belonged to.

Parasaurolophus

PA-ra-sore-OL-off-us

12

Velociraptor

veh-LOSS-ee-rap-tuhr

17

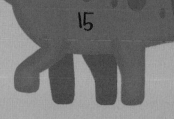

Diplodocus

dip-LOH-doh-kus

15

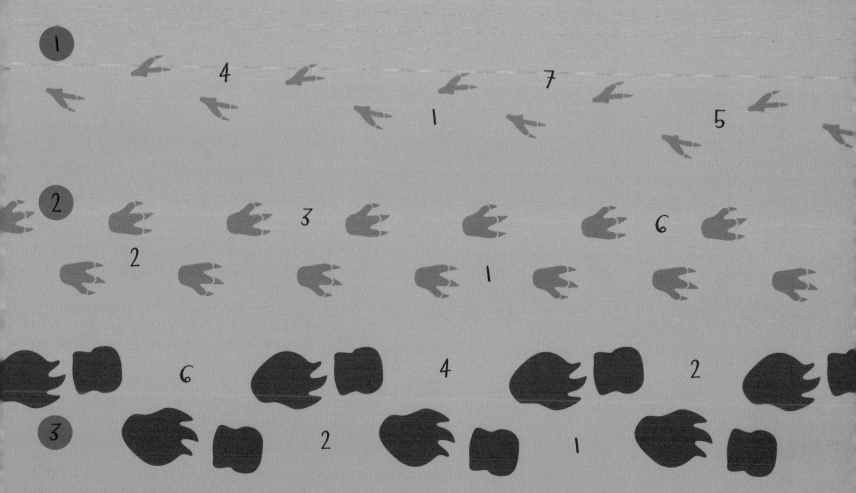

1   4   7   1   5

2   3   2   6   1

3   6   4   2   2   1

FAMILIAR FACES

Some creatures that shared the Earth with dinosaurs are still around today!

Unscramble the letters to discover their names, and write them in the boxes.

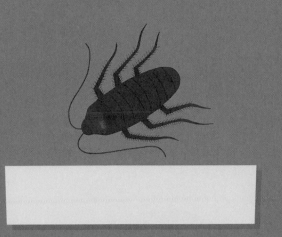

EBE

HROHSESOE CARB

RHKSA

CKROOHACC

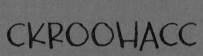

COPY-SAURUS REX

Use the grid to copy this image of a Tyrannosaurus rex square by square!

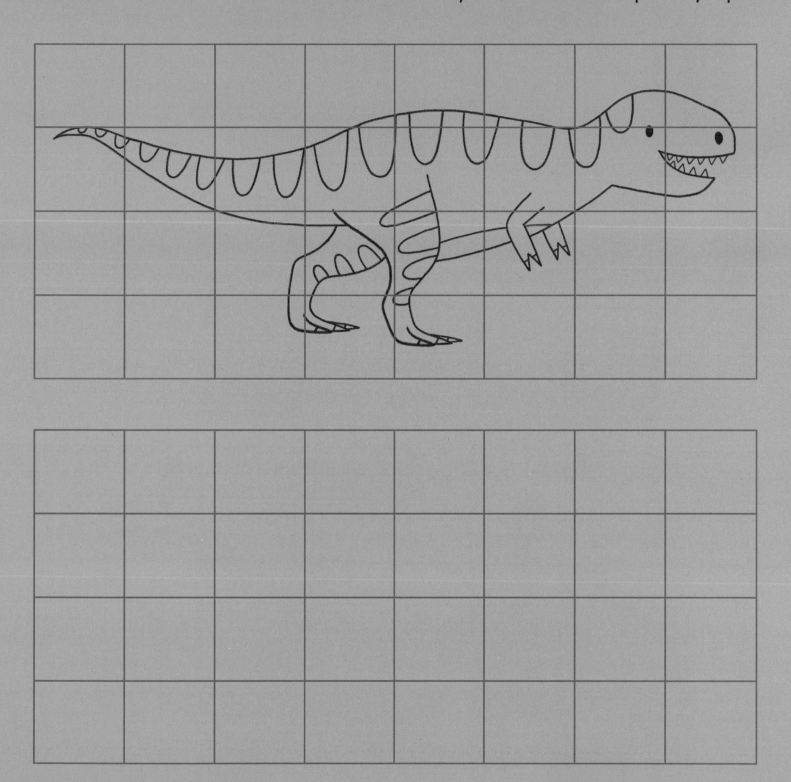

ty-RAN-oh-SORE-us REX

GIANT OF THE SKIES

Quetzalcoatlus was the largest creature ever to take to the sky! It had a whopping wingspan that measured nearly 11 m (36 ft).

Starting at A4, plot the flight of this Quetzalcoatlus to see which square it ends up in.

Start at A4; Down 2; Right 5; Up 3; Left 2; Up 2; Right 1; Down 5

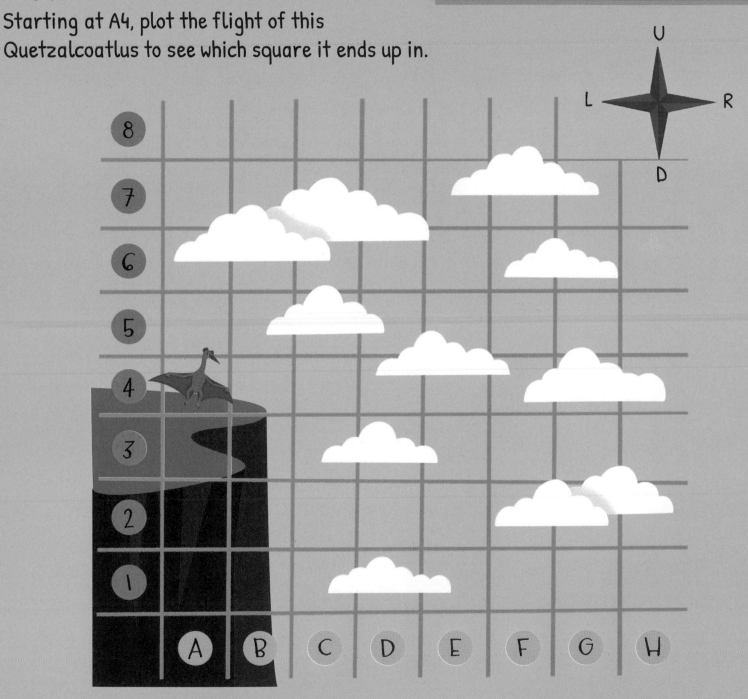

KWETS-ul-koh-AT-lus

DEINONYCHUS SPOT

Deinonychus might have hunted in groups for large animals but caught smaller animals alone.

Can you spot all five differences between these two pictures of a Deinonychus on the prowl?

dy-NON-ik-us

CAIHONG CODE

Caihong was a birdlike dinosaur.
Scientists think it had bright, shiny feathers.

Use this key to recreate what this Jurassic creature might have looked like!

1 2 3 4 5 6

kai-HONG

STYRACOSAURUS COUNT UP

Styracosaurus is an impressive-looking relative of Triceratops. Its wide frill might have been used to attract a mate or scare away predators.

How many Styracosaurus can you count on this page?

sty-RACK-oh-SORE-us

BARELY BARYONYX

Baryonyx lived in the early Cretaceous Period, and its head was similar in shape to a crocodile's.

Take a look at the pieces of this Baryonyx's markings. Which ones complete the picture?

A   B   C   D   E   F

BAH-ree-ON-icks

FIRST FINDINGS

The first dinosaur bone was investigated by Robert Plot in 1677, although at the time he thought it was the bone of a human giant! It would be almost 200 years before the first complete dinosaur skeleton was put together.

7957?1*&3?6,   8#3c61   !3#2174

Use the codebreaker to discover where this first bone was found.

D	E	F	G	H	I	K	M	N	O	R	S	T	U	X	Y	B	A
1	6	5	2	&	3	!	4	#	7	?	*	c	8	9	+	<	[

Write the answer here.

WING WORKING OUT

Dimorphodon was a type of pterosaur that lived in the Jurassic Period and has been found in Southern England.

Take a look at these flying Dimorphodons, then draw a line between the equations and their answers.

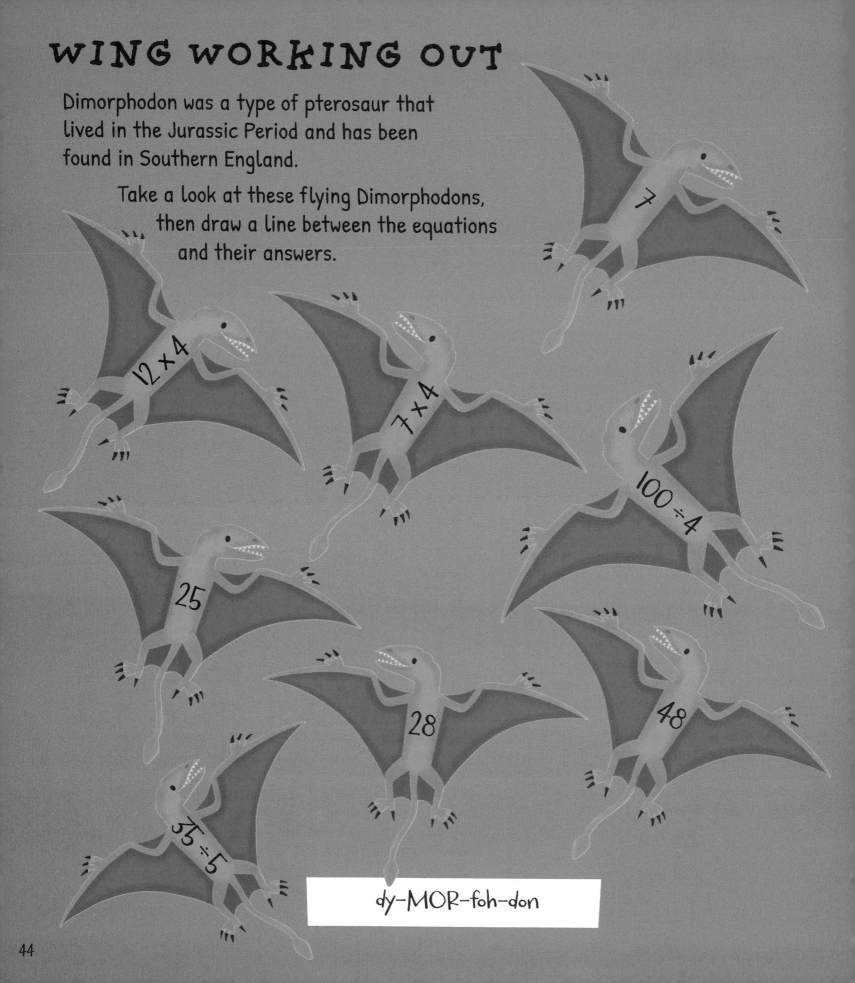

7

12×4

7×4

$100 \div 4$

25

28

48

$35 \div 5$

dy-MOR-foh-don

PROTOCERATOPS PROWL

Protoceratops lived in a part of the world that was hot and dry during the Cretaceous Period, so it would have to work hard to find a leafy meal!

Start

Help guide this Protoceratops through the maze.

Finish

PRO-toh-SEH-rah-tops

SHADOW-SAURS

Allosaurus looked something like Tyrannosaurus rex but lived 80-90 million years earlier.

Can you find the silhouette that matches this Allosaurus?

AL-oh-SORE-us

TIME PERIOD PUZZLE

Can you find all of these prehistoric time periods in the grid below? Each word can go forward, backward, vertically, and even diagonally!

Jurassic   Triassic   Cretaceous   Mesozoic   Cenozoic

A	S	G	H	B	N	X	C	V	G
C	I	S	S	A	R	U	J	G	M
D	F	V	C	B	G	G	R	E	E
R	R	A	S	G	F	B	N	N	S
T	R	I	A	S	S	I	C	U	O
F	R	E	D	B	H	M	O	E	Z
F	G	V	B	X	C	E	W	E	O
C	F	G	V	B	C	R	E	D	I
H	G	B	N	A	B	N	M	A	C
F	G	H	T	J	U	K	O	L	P
E	R	E	T	Y	H	U	M	K	L
R	R	B	H	N	J	U	Y	F	K
C	A	C	E	N	O	Z	O	I	C

47

A MEGA MUSEUM

We can see what scientists have learned about dinosaurs by visiting museums.

Take a look at this picture of a busy museum, and see if you can spot all the details.

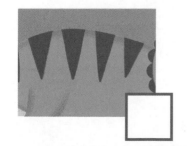

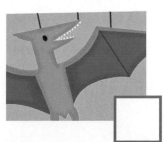

DILOPHOSAURUS DOTS

Dilophosaurus was a very interesting-looking dinosaur.

Starting at 1, follow the dots to finish off this picture, and see for yourself!

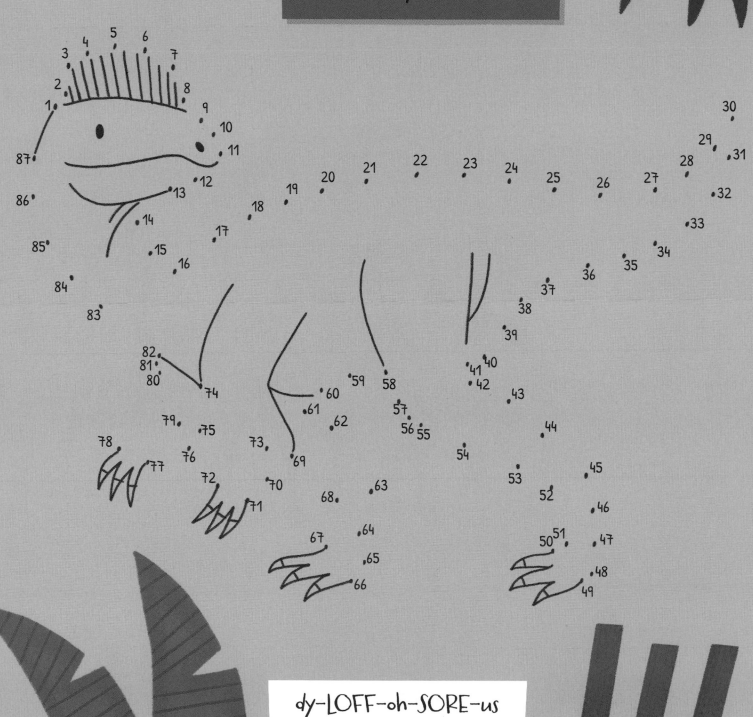

dy-LOFF-oh-SORE-us

STRANGE, BUT TRUE?

Rhinorex was a hadrosaur with an enlarged nose.

Can you guess which of these facts are true and which are false?

Rhinorex was discovered in 2014.

T ☐ F ☐

Its name means "nose king."

T ☐ F ☐

It roamed very dry areas.

T ☐ F ☐

It liked swampy areas.

T ☐ F ☐

It only ate plants.

T ☐ F ☐

It only ate meat.

T ☐ F ☐

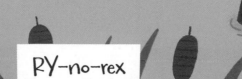

RY-no-rex

MODERN-DAY DESCENDANT!

Believe it or not, the common chicken is related to one of the most recognizable dinosaurs ever!

Follow the lines to discover which one.

Diplodocus
dip-LOH-doh-kus

Tyrannosaurus rex
ty-RAN-oh-SORE-us REX

Triceratops
try-SEH-ra-tops

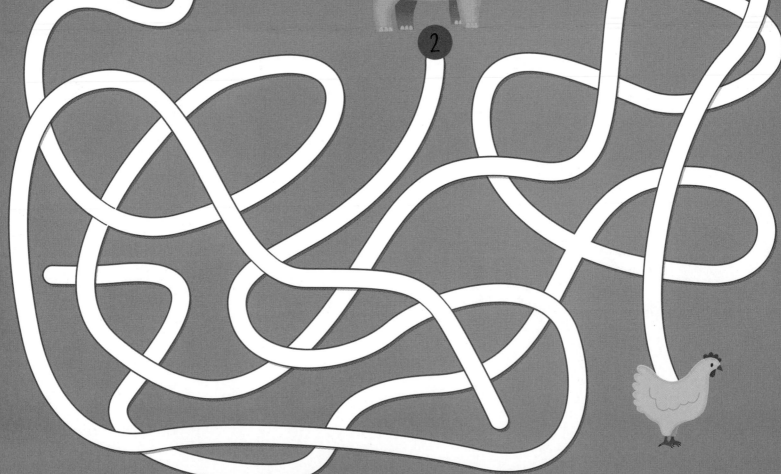

MIRROR IMAGE

This Hadrosaurus has found a cool river to take a drink from.

Take a look at the reflections to see if you can find the Hadrosaur's correct mirror image.

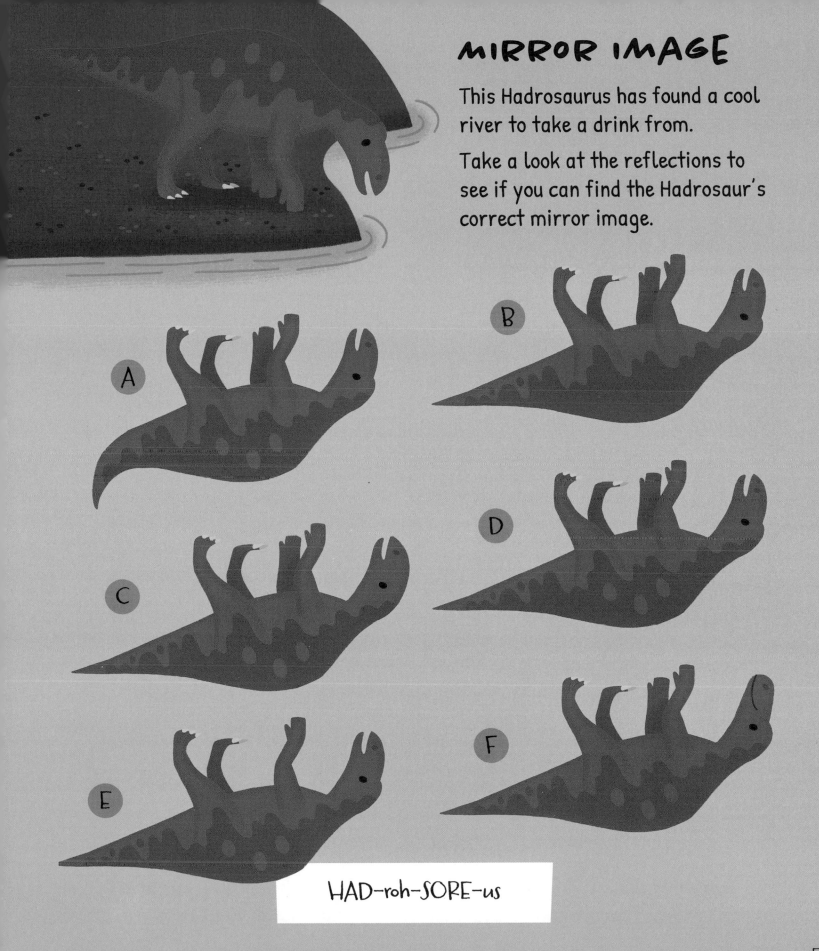

HAD-roh-SORE-us

TOTALLY TRUE!

Can you match each animal to the fun fact?
Draw a line to match each fact to a name.

Ichthyosaurus

ICK-thee-oh-SORE-us

1

This dinosaur had two rows of kite-shaped plates sticking out from its back.

2

This dinosaur had a razor-sharp curved claw on each foot.

Velociraptor

veh-LOSS-ee-rap-tuhr

3

Mary Anning discovered this sea-dwelling reptile's fossil in around 1840.

4

This is thought to be the heaviest dinosaur ever found. It weighed the same as 17 African elephants!

Argentinosaurus

AR-juhn-TEE-no-SORE-us

Stegosaurus

STEG-oh-SORE-us

BARE BONES

We know what dinosaurs might have looked like based on the bones that have been found.

Try matching these prehistoric reptiles to their fossilized bones.

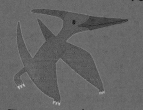

Pteranodon

A

Stegosaurus

B

Diplodocus

C

Triceratops

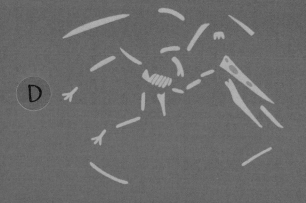

D

PREHISTORIC PLANTS

Some trees and plants we see today have been around since prehistoric times.

Can you place each one of these plants in the grid, once in each row, column, and minigrid?

Ginkgo tree   Cyad plant   Allspice flower   Magnolia

SHADOW-CASTER

We have found fossils from only one Banji dinosaur. Banji lived in the late Cretaceous Period and looked a lot like the birds we see today.

Take a look at this Banji. Can you find its matching silhouette below?

BAHN-jee

WHICH SEA REPTILE CAME FIRST?

Prehistoric oceans were full of amazing creatures that lived millions of years ago.

Follow the lines to discover which order these incredible creatures came in and what period they belonged to.

Liopleurodon

LY-oh-PLOO-ro-don

Albertonectes

AI-BER-toe-NEK-teez

TRIASSIC

JURASSIC

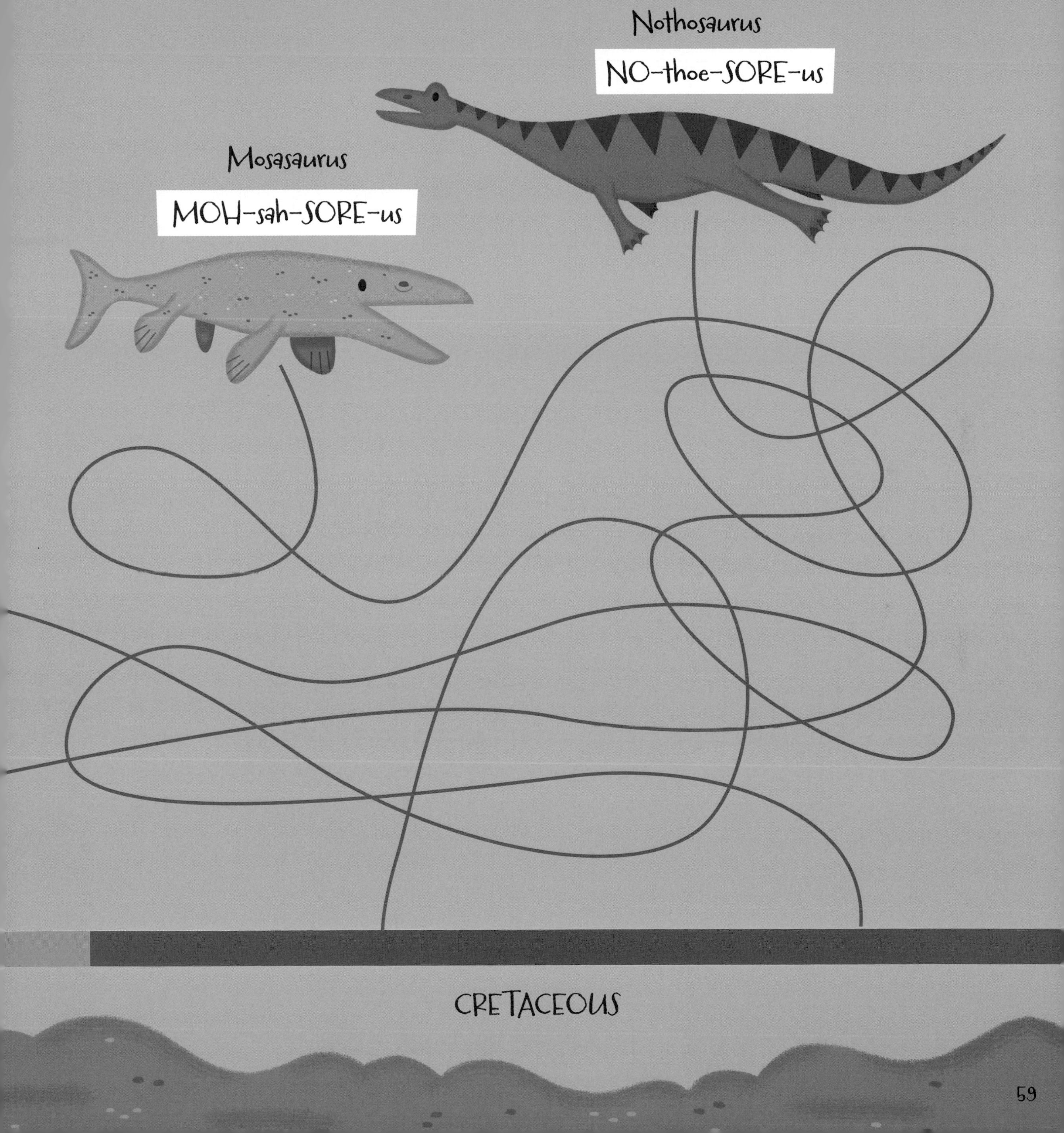

Nothosaurus

NO-thoe-SORE-us

Mosasaurus

MOH-sah-SORE-us

CRETACEOUS

ODD NODOSAURUS OUT!

Nodosaurus had tough spikes to defend itself from predators!

Take a look at these pictures of Nodosaurus. Can you pick out which one is different from the rest?

NOH-doh-SORE-us

STRENGTH IN NUMBERS

Camptosaurus and Stegosaurus lived at the same time in the same locations. They probably lived peacefully alongside one another.

Can you find the missing pieces to complete this picture?

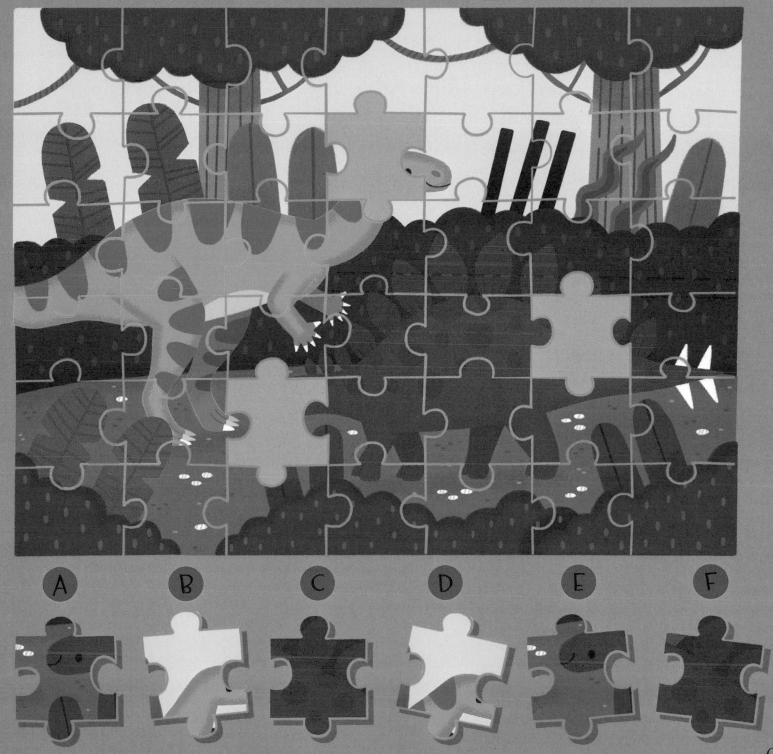

ART WITH WINGS

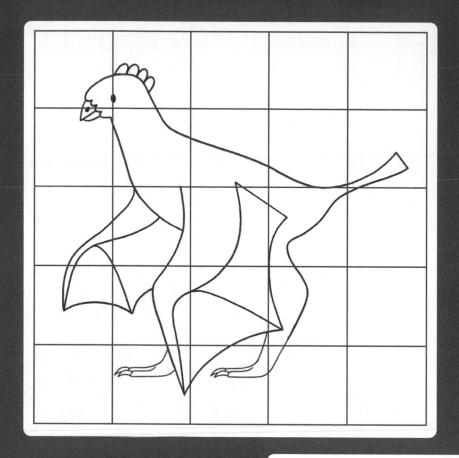

The flying Yi dinosaur looks similar to the birds we see today.

Use the grid to copy the picture.

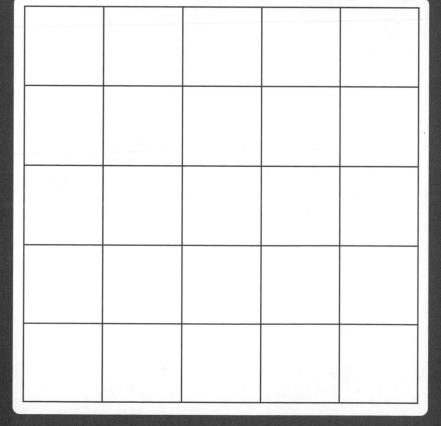

Yee

EXTINCTION EVENT

Take a look at this picture, and rearrange the panels in the correct number order. The first and last panels should stay where they are.

Scientists believe that the sudden disappearance of dinosaurs 66 million years ago was the result of a massive asteroid hitting Earth, wiping out 75 percent of all species on the planet.

WHO'S THAT REPTILE?

This fearsome reptile looked like a stocky crocodile that could walk on two legs!

Using the codebreaker opposite, crack the code below to discover its name.

Codebreaker

C	D	H	O	P	S	T	N	U
○	→	❋	●	□	★	◆	◉	✹

Write the answer here.

64

HAPPY EATERS

Some dinosaurs ate only meat, some ate only plants, and some ate both!

Sort these dinosaurs into meat-eaters and plant-eaters based on their characteristics.

Spinosaurus

SPINE-oh-SORE-us

Ankylosaurus

an-KIH-loh-SORE-us

Allosaurus

AL-oh-SORE-us

Brachiosaurus

BRAK-ee-oh-SORE-us

Qianzhousaurus

chi-an-sue-SORE-us

Write the answers here.

Meat –Eaters Sharp teeth, sharp claws, fast	Plant-Eaters Flat teeth, rounded feet, slow

QUIRKY CREST!

Lambeosaurus' unusual crest could have had many different functions. It might have been to help with communication, to boost its sense of smell, or simply to impress other dinosaurs!

Can you see six differences between these two pictures?

lam-BEE-oh-SORE-us

TRICERATOPS TRICKS

Take a look at this Triceratops' nesting site for 30 seconds, then turn the page to see if you can answer all the questions.

try-SEH-ra-tops

How many of these questions can you answer without peeking back a page?

1. How many eggs were in the middle nest?

2. How many adult Triceratops were in the picture?

3. Were the flowers pink or purple?

4. How many hatchlings were in the right-hand nest?

5. How many hatchlings were in the left-hand nest?

MAKE YOUR OWN DISCOVERY

New dinosaurs are being discovered all the time, with mysteries still to be solved. Imagine you have uncovered a brand-new dinosaur, and draw it in the space below.

Here are some ideas to get you started:

Would it stand on two legs or four?

Would it have bright markings, feathers, a beak, or snout?

Would it be a meat-eater or a plant-eater?

Don't forget to give it a name, too!

PACHYCEPHALOSAURUS PARALLELS

Pachycephalosaurus is known for its big skull. Its name means "thick-headed lizard."

Take a look at this picture, then see if you can find its exact reflection.

A

B

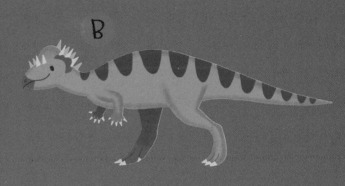

C

D

E

pack-ee-SEF-ah-lo-SORE-us

SLOW TRAFFIC AHEAD!

Sauropelta was probably one of the slowest dinosaurs.

Help this dino find the fastest route from start to finish.

Start

A

4 seconds

D

2 seconds

3 seconds

5 seconds

2 seconds

C

2 seconds

E

4 seconds

B

5 seconds

Finish

2 seconds

SORE-oh-PELT-ah

STEGOSAURUS STENCIL

Stegosaurus lived in the late Jurassic Period. Its name means "roof lizard."

Use the grid below to draw your own Stegosaurus!

STEG-oh-SORE-us

A VERY LONG SHADOW!

Diplodocus was a type of sauropod—the tallest dinosaur to roam the Earth! Diplodocus could reach up to 4.6 m (15 ft) tall from shoulder to the ground.

Which of these silhouettes matches the Diplodocus perfectly?

dip-LOH-doh-kus

MOUNTAIN RANGER

Scientists think that Edmontonia could have lived in the mountains because fossils have been found in the Edmonton Formation in the foothills of the Rockies.

Can you help this Edmontonia through the mountain range?

Start

Finish

ED-mon-TONE-ee-ah

HATCHING TIME!

Many dinosaurs probably laid their eggs on the ground. Some may have made nests in mounds of earth.

Figure out these equations, then cross off each answer as you find it. The remaining egg will be the one that hatches first!

$$21 + 37$$

$$6 \times 8$$

$$72 \div 6$$

$$98 - 56$$

$$6 \times 9$$

42   12   58

54   48   39

WHICH FLYING REPTILE CAME FIRST?

Soaring high in the air, these winged reptiles would have ruled the skies!

Complete each equation to calculate the position of each animal on the timeline, then draw them in place.

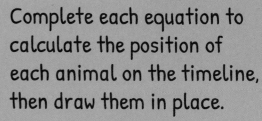

Quetzalcoatlus

KWETS-ul-koh-AT-lus

$6 \times 8 - 43 =$

Pteranodon

teh-RAH-no-don

$100 - 71 - 25 =$

1

2

EARLY	MIDDLE	LATE	

TRIASSIC   JURASSIC

Confuciusornis

KON-few-shus-OR-nis

$7 \times 9 - 60 =$

Eudimorphodon

YOU-di-MOR-fo-don

$512 - 25 - 71 - 415 =$

Anchiornis

AN-kee-OR-niss

$12 \times 5 - 58 =$

3

4

5

EARLY

LATE

CRETACEOUS

ARGENTINOSAURUS

Argentinosaurus is the largest dinosaur to be discovered. To get to its gigantic size, it would grow by 40 kg (88 lb) a day! Despite all we know about its size, dinosaur scientists still don't know what its markings were like.

Finish this picture with what you believe Argentinosaurus looked like.

AR-juhn-TEE-no-SORE-us

SOLO EUROPASAURUS!

Europasaurus is one of the smallest known sauropods.

Can you find the dinosaur that doesn't quite match the others?

YOO-roh-pah-SORE-us

SKULL SKILLS

The first Triceratops was discovered all the way back in 1887—but scientists thought it was a type of bison at first!

Can you match these Triceratops skulls into pairs?

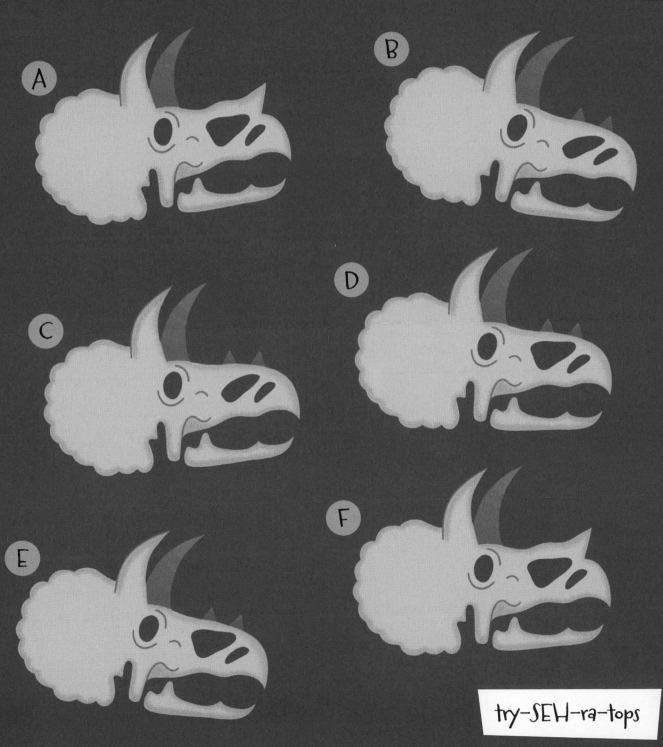

try-SEH-ra-tops

80

FOLLOW THE TRAIL

Follow the dinosaur footprints in sequence from start to finish. You can move up, down, left, and right, but not diagonally.

Start

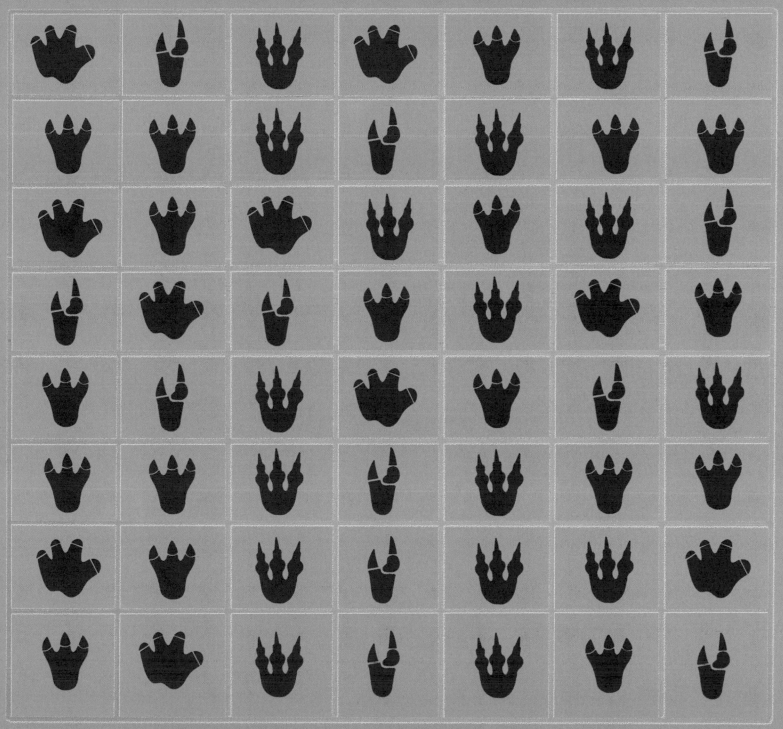

Finish

ORDER, ORDER!

The strange Nipponites had twisting, coiled shells.

Take a look at this picture and rearrange the panels in the correct number order. The first and last panels should stay where they are.

nih-pon-AYE-tes

BRONTOSAURUS LUNCH

Brontosaurus liked to munch on ferns called horsetails. Take a look at this patch, and see if you can find the horsetail fern that perfectly matches the picture opposite to give this Brontosaurus her next meal!

Horsetail Fern

BRONT-uh-SORE-us

SNACK TIME

Coloradisaurus ate a mixture of plants and possibly insects.

Fit the jigsaw puzzle pieces in the correct places. Which pieces don't belong?

A   B   C   D   E   F

KOH-loh-rah-dih-SORE-us

SPEEDY DRYOSAURUS

Dryosaurus lived in the Jurassic period and was a small herbivore with strong back legs.

Starting at A1, plot the Dryosaurus' route to see where he ends up on the map.

Start at A1; Up 5; Right 5; Down 2; Left 4; Down 2; Right 5; Up 6

DRY-oh-SORE-us

SHINING SHONISAURUS

Shonisaurus could grow up to 21 m (just over 69 ft) long. Scientists believe that only the young had teeth. Adults didn't need them because they preferred eating soft things like squid.

Take a look at this scene of swimming Shonisaurus. Can you find all the items on the list?

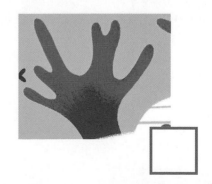

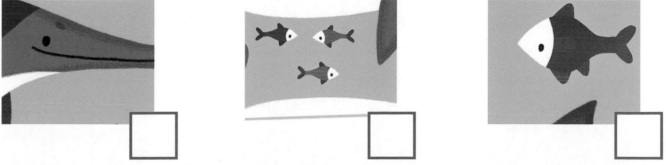

PICK A PISANOSAURUS

Pisanosaurus was a small, plant-eating dinosaur about the size of a cat.

How many can you count on the page?

PEE-san-oh-SORE-us

DISCOVERED!

Follow the lines to find out where each of these dinosaurs was discovered for the first time!

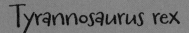

Tyrannosaurus rex

ty-RAN-oh-SORE-us REX

Spinosaurus

SPINE-oh-SORE-us

Iguanodon

ig-WAH-noh-don

Egypt

United States

United Kingdom

SOLUTIONS

Page 3

Pages 4-5

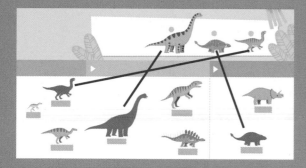

Page 6

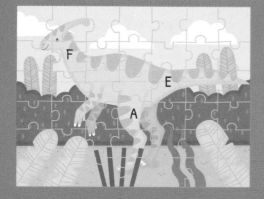

Page 7
The mother Heyuannia huangi should take route B.

Page 8

Page 9

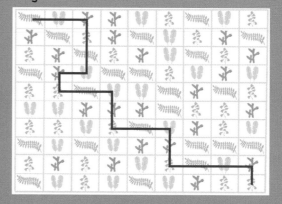

Page 10

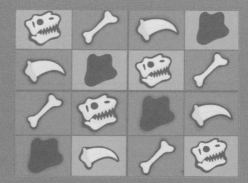

Page 11
The three matching pairs are A & E; B & F; C & D.

Pages 12-13

Page 14
There are nine Microraptors.

Page 15
The Plesiosaurus will eat 29 fish along the way.

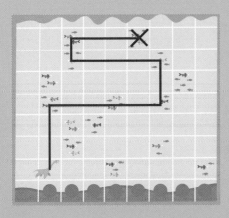

Page 16
AMMONITE

Page 18
The first fossils to be discovered were their teeth. TRUE
They could jump as high as a house. FALSE
They could swim. FALSE
They each weighed as much as a small truck. TRUE
They only ate brown leaves. FALSE

Page 19
G is the odd one out.

Pages 20-21
Order of oldest to most recent:
Plateosaurus
Cryolophosaurus
Diplodocus
Achillobator

Page 22

Page 23
The fastest route is A B F G.

Page 24
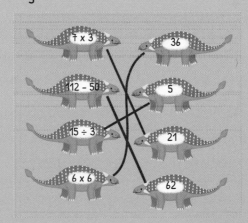

Page 25
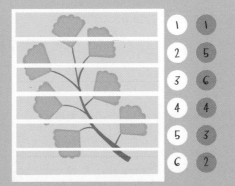

Page 26

Pages 27–28
1. How many blue pencils were there? Two
2. Was the notebook open or closed? Open
3. What was the fossil brush blue or green? Green
4. How many bones were being uncovered? One
5. Was the trowel handle red or yellow? Yellow

Page 29
5 is the Elasmosaurus that isn't quite like the others.

Page 30

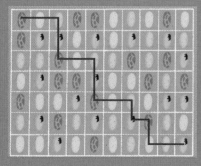

Page 31
Chasmosaurus is the horned dinosaur being described.

Page 32
Skeleton 3 is an exact match.

Page 33
There are 12 Ankylosaurus teeth and 10 Spinosaurus teeth.
Match the descriptions:
These long, sharp teeth allowed its carnivorous owner to tear through the flesh of its prey. SPINOSAURUS TOOTH
These belonged to a herbivore. The small, leaf-shaped teeth were designed for chewing plants. ANKYLOSAURUS TOOTH

Page 34

Page 35
1. Velcociraptor
2. Parasaurolophus
3. Diplodocus

Page 36

BEE   HORSESHOE CRAB   SHARK   COCKROACH

Page 38
The Quetzalcoatlus ends up in square E2.

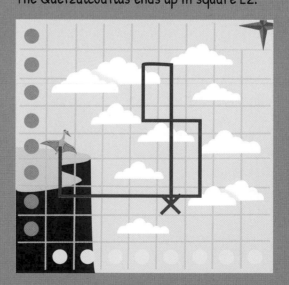

Page 39

Page 40

Page 41
There are 12 Stryracosaurus.

Page 42

Page 43
The first dinosaur bone was found in OXFORDSHIRE, UNITED KINGDOM.

Page 44

Page 45

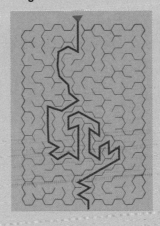

Page 46
Silhouette D

Page 47

A	S	G	H	B	N	X	C	V	G
C	I	S	S	A	R	U	J	G	M
D	F	V	C	B	G	G	R	E	E
R	R	A	S	G	F	B	N	N	S
T	R	I	A	S	S	I	C	U	O
F	R	E	D	B	H	M	O	E	Z
F	G	V	B	X	C	E	W	E	O
C	F	G	V	B	C	R	E	D	I
H	G	B	N	A	B	N	M	A	C
F	G	H	T	J	U	K	O	L	P
E	R	E	T	Y	H	U	M	K	L
R	R	B	H	N	J	U	Y	F	K
C	A	C	E	N	O	Z	O	I	C

Pages 48–49

Page 50

Page 51
Rhinorex was discovered in 2014. TRUE
Its name means "nose king." TRUE
It roamed very dry areas. FALSE
It liked swampy areas. TRUE
It only ate plants. TRUE
It only ate meat. FALSE

Page 52
1. Tyrannosaurus rex is related to the common chicken.

Page 53
D is the true mirror image of the Hadrosaurus.

Page 54
1. Stegosaurus
2. Velociraptor
3. Ichthyosaurus
4. Argentinosaurus

Page 55
Pteranodon—D
Stegosaurus—C
Diplodocus—B
Triceratops—A

Page 56

Page 57
E is the true silhouette image of the Banji dinosaur.

Pages 58–59
Creatures in order of time period they lived in:
Triassic—Nothosaurus
Jurassic—Liopleurodon
Cretaceous—Albertonectes; Mosasaurus

Page 60
E is the Nodosaurus that is different from the rest.

Page 61

Page 63

Page 64
POSTOSUCHUS (POST-oh-SOOK-us)

Page 65
Meat-Eaters   Plant-Eaters
Spinosaurus   Ankylosaurus
Allosaurus   Brachiosaurus
Qianzhousaurus

Page 66

Pages 67-68
1. How many eggs were in the middle nest? Seven
2. How many adult Triceratops were in the picture? Four
3. Was the dinosaur with its eyes closed pink or purple? Purple
4. How many hatchlings were in the right-hand nest? Three
5. How many hatchlings were in the left-hand nest? None

Page 70
C is the exact reflection of the Pachycephalosaurus.

Page 71
The fastest route is A C E.

Page 73
Silhouette B matches the Diplodocus perfectly.

Page 74

Page 75
6 x 8 = 48
21 + 37 = 58
98 − 56 = 42
72 ÷ 6 = 12
6 x 9 = 54
39 is the egg that will hatch first.

Pages 76-77
1. Eudimorphodon
2. Anchiornis
3. Confuciusornis
4. Pteranodon
5. Quetzalcoatlus

Page 79
D is the dinosaur that doesn't quite match the others.

Page 80
Matching pairs: A&F, B&C, D&E

Page 81

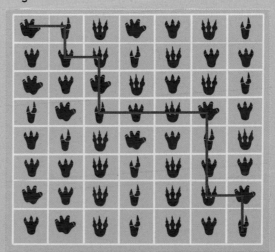

Page 82

1	2	3	4	5	6	7	8	9	10	11	12
1	5	3	7	2	6	9	11	4	8	10	12

Page 83

Page 84

Pieces C, E, and F don't belong.

Page 85

The Dryosaurus ends up in square G8.

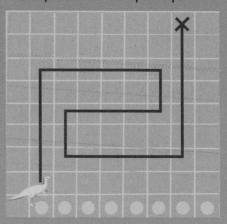

Pages 86–87

Page 88

There are 19 Pisanosaurus.

Page 89

Tyrannosaurus rex—United States
Iguanodon—United Kingdom
Spinosaurus—Egypt